D0513280

puddings

Rick Stein puddings

Published by BBC Books, BBC Worldwide Ltd,
Woodlands, 80 Wood Lane, London W12 0TT

First published 2004
Reprinted 2005 (twice)
Copyright © Rick Stein 2004
The moral right of the author has been asserted

Food photography © James Murphy 2002 and
2004. Location photography © Craig Easton 2000
Portrait of Rick Stein and Chalky on page 6
© David Pritchard 1999

The recipes in this book first appeared in the
following titles: **Fruits of the Sea**, **Food Heroes** and
Food Heroes: Another Helping, which were
originally published by BBC Worldwide in 1997,
2002 and 2004 respectively.

ISBN 0 563 52191 0

Commissioning Editor: Vivien Bowler
Project Editors: Rachel Copus and Warren Albers
Designer: Andrew Barron
Production Controller: Kenneth McKay
Food Stylist: Debbie Major

Set in Din and Veljovic
Printed and bound in Singapore
Colour separations by Butler and Tanner Ltd

Jacket photography:
Food photography and portrait of Rick Stein
© James Murphy 2004
Landscape photography © Craig Easton 2000

contents

There's a lot to read in most cookery books. Sometimes I think one is spoiled for choice. Guided by the theory that 'less is more', I thought that three books each containing a dozen or so recipes covering first courses, main courses and puddings would be a welcome alternative. So I've compiled three mini cookery books, choosing the recipes from the nine books I've written to give the widest possible range of dishes that best illustrate my personal style of cooking. I like to think of them as my 'best of' recipe collections.

To illustrate this, I joke with the producer of my TV series, David Pritchard, that most of his CD collection seems to be labelled 'The best of'. I call him Compilation Man, which hurts him a little because actually he has a very acute knowledge of music. But sometimes a slim volume of 'best of' dishes like this sets a boundary on cooking at a time when you might be suffering from information overload.

I have fanciful thoughts that these would be all you need, say, on holiday, cooking in a rented house or villa. You could slip these slim volumes into your luggage and be armed with a repertoire of enough dishes to deal with a light lunch over a glass of wine, supper for the children or a serious dinner for a party of friends.

Looking through the recipes, I can't help feeling that it's actually quite a good 'repertoire' of puddings. There's a couple of popular nursery puddings in the **Caramelised bread-and-butter pudding** and the **Steamed treacle sponge**. There are two delicious tarts in the **Walnut tart** (which is like a Bakewell tart, but much more interesting) and the **Classic lemon tart**. There are two British classics in the **White wine syllabub** and the **Traditional English trifle**, and a moist, dark **Sunken chocolate cake**, which only a half bottle of Australian Rutherglen Muscat can partner. I considered adding raspberries and ice cream to the selection, or strawberries, double cream and caster sugar – which for me is almost more about the cream and sugar than the strawberries – but these hardly qualify as recipes.

I couldn't, however, put together a selection like this without including rhubarb somewhere. It was a difficult decision to leave out rhubarb crumble, but then I already had two British puddings, so I chose **Panna cotta with stewed rhubarb**. I think the panna cotta recipe is very delicately balanced, using only enough gelatine to set it, thus allowing it to retain the sensation of being just 'cooked milk'.

I chose most of these recipes by virtue of the frequency I cook them myself. This applies particularly to the **Light apple tart with quince purée**, which came from Joyce Molyneux, who was chef and part owner of The Carved Angel restaurant in Dartmouth. She had an amazing aptitude for English cooking, making it seem a very sophisticated but friendly cuisine. However, I suspect her food had a lot more to do with her interpretation of things than anything handed down. The quince purée adds a unique and delicious, almost smoky-sweet taste to the tart, but I've included a note about apple purée too as quinces are very seasonal. You can also, of course, leave out the purée altogether.

Like most people these days I'm quite easy about buying in what I need for a dish as long as it's good enough; a sheet or two of frozen puff pastry layered with thinly sliced apples, sprinkled with sugar and baked, then brushed with melted apricot jam and served with crème fraîche is just about perfection in a sweet and so easy to do.

The **Beignets soufflés** are almost always on the menu at my Seafood Restaurant in Cornwall. Sweets like this are where my heart really lies – uncomplicated, yet requiring the best materials: free-range eggs for the choux paste, fresh oil for the deep-frying, and good dark chocolate.

If it's not something freshly made, I tend to favour light sweets such as the **Panna cotta** or **Black-rice pudding with mango sorbet**. Black rice is much used in Asia for sweet dishes and has recently swept through smart restaurants in Australia, whence this recipe comes. You can buy it in the UK from Asian food stores or any good deli. It has a pleasing *al dente* quality, even when long cooked. This is a great favourite of mine at the Seafood Restaurant; it's not at all filling and I'm very fond of the combination of mango and coconut.

Lastly, I must make mention of **Pavlova with cream and passion fruit**. This is another Australian dish and, though pavlova has long been associated with strawberries, it is far nicer when made with this more appropriate local fruit. The meringue is marshmallow-like in the centre and the whole thing is a triumph of fragility, created by the addition of cornflour and vinegar to the egg white.

puddings

pavlova with cream and passion fruit

SERVES 8

6 egg whites
350 g (12 oz) caster sugar
2 teaspoons cornflour
1 teaspoon white wine vinegar
A pinch of salt
600 ml (1 pint) double cream, to serve
8 passion fruit, to serve

1 Preheat the oven to 140°C/275°F/Gas Mark 1. Lightly grease 1 large or 2 smaller baking trays and line with non-stick baking paper.

2 In a large bowl, whisk the egg whites with a pinch of salt into stiff peaks. Gradually whisk in the sugar to make a very stiff and shiny meringue. Whisk in the cornflour and vinegar.

3 Drop 8 large spoonfuls of the mixture on to the baking tray(s) and spread each one into a 10 cm (4 in) round. Bake for 45 minutes until pale in colour and marshmallow-like in the centre. Turn off the oven, leave the door ajar and leave them to cool.

4 To serve, whip the cream into soft peaks. Spoon some into the centre of each pavlova and spread it out very slightly. Halve the passion fruit and spoon the pulp over the cream. Serve within 5 minutes.

walnut tart

SERVES 10-12

**1 quantity Rich shortcrust
pastry (see page 40)**
3 tablespoons raspberry jam
225 g (8 oz) walnut pieces
50 g (2 oz) plain flour
225 g (8 oz) softened butter
225 g (8 oz) caster sugar
3 medium eggs, beaten
1 teaspoon vanilla extract
Icing sugar, for dusting
Crème fraîche, to serve

1 Roll out the pastry on a lightly floured surface and use to line a 4 cm (1½ in) deep, 25 cm (10 in) loose-bottomed flan tin. Spread the base of the case with the jam and chill for 30 minutes.

2 Preheat the oven to 180°C/350°F/Gas Mark 4. Put the walnuts into a food processor and grind briefly until chopped. Then add the flour and blend briefly once more into a fine mixture, but don't overdo it or the walnuts will go oily.

3 Cream the butter and the sugar together until pale and fluffy. Gradually beat in the beaten eggs, add the vanilla extract and then gently fold in the walnut mixture. Spread it into the pastry case, taking the mixture right up to the edges, and bake in the oven for 50-55 minutes or until springy to the touch and when a skewer, pushed into the centre, comes out clean. Cover with a double sheet of greaseproof paper towards the end of cooking if it starts to get too brown. Remove from the oven and leave to cool.

4 Remove the tart from the tin and dust it with icing sugar. Cut it into wedges and serve with some crème fraîche.

sunken chocolate cake

SERVES 8

225 g (8 oz) butter
225 g (8 oz) good-quality
plain chocolate,
broken into pieces
50 g (2 oz) ground almonds
60 g (2¼ oz) plain flour
6 medium eggs, at
room temperature
50 g (2 oz) light soft
brown sugar
175 g (6 oz) caster sugar
Icing sugar, for dusting
Double cream, to serve

1 Preheat the oven to 180°C/350°F/Gas Mark 4. Grease a 20 cm (8 in) clip-sided cake tin and line with baking paper.

2 Put the butter and chocolate into a heatproof bowl and rest it over a pan of barely simmering water. Leave until melted, then stir until smooth. Remove and leave to cool slightly.

3 Sift together the ground almonds and flour. Separate the eggs into 2 large bowls. Add the light brown sugar to the egg yolks and whisk until pale and creamy. Gently fold in the melted chocolate mixture, followed by the almond and flour mixture.

4 Whisk the egg whites into soft peaks and then whisk in the caster sugar, a little at a time, to make a soft meringue. If it's too stiff you will find it difficult to fold into the rest of the cake mixture. Fold it in with a large metal spoon, pour the mixture into the prepared tin and bake for 50 minutes or until a skewer, inserted into the cake, comes out still a bit wet. This cake is best if slightly undercooked. Remove from the oven and leave to cool.

5 Carefully remove from the tin and pull off the paper. Cut into wedges, dust with icing sugar and serve with some pouring cream.

beignets soufflés with chocolate sauce

SERVES 6

75 g (3 oz) butter
225 ml (7½ fl oz) cold water
95 g (3¾ oz) plain flour,
well sifted
3 large eggs, beaten
Sunflower oil, for deep-frying
50 g (2 oz) caster sugar
¾ teaspoon ground cinnamon
1 quantity Chocolate sauce
(see page 42)

1 For the beignets, put the butter and water into a pan and leave over a low heat until the butter has melted. Turn up the heat, bring to the boil and then add the flour and beat vigorously until the mixture is smooth and leaves the sides of the pan. Leave to cool slightly and then gradually beat in the eggs to make a smooth, glossy choux pastry.

2 Heat a large pan of oil for deep-frying to 190°C/375°F. Drop about 6–8 heaped teaspoons of the choux pastry into the oil, taking care not to overcrowd the pan, and cook for 5 minutes, turning them over now and then, until they are puffed up, crisp and golden. Don't be tempted to lift them out too soon – they will continue to expand in size as they cook for the full 5 minutes, which allows sufficient time for the choux pastry in the centre to cook. Lift them out with a slotted spoon on to a tray lined with kitchen paper and drain briefly, then keep hot in a low oven while you cook the rest.

3 Mix the caster sugar and cinnamon together in a shallow dish, add the beignets, a few at a time, and toss them gently until they are well coated.

4 To serve, arrange 4 of the beignets in the centre of large, warm plates and drizzle some of the chocolate sauce over and around them. Serve immediately while still warm.

SERVES 8

175 g (6 oz) softened butter,
plus a little extra
for greasing
175 g (6 oz) light
muscovado sugar
1 tablespoon black treacle
3 large eggs
175 g (6 oz) self-raising flour
1 quantity each Butterscotch
sauce (see page 42) and
Custard (see page 41)

1 Generously grease a 1.2 litre (2 pint) pudding basin with some butter. Cream the butter in a bowl until light and creamy. Add the muscovado sugar and beat vigorously until the mixture is pale and fluffy, then beat in the black treacle. Beat in the eggs one at a time, adding a large spoonful of the flour with the last egg, and then gently fold in the rest of the flour.

2 Spoon the mixture into the pudding basin and lightly level the top of the mixture. Cover the bowl with a pleated sheet of buttered foil and tie in place with string.

3 Bring 5 cm (2 in) of water to the boil in a large pan containing some sort of shallow trivet in the base. Add the pudding, cover and steam for 2 hours.

4 Make the butterscotch sauce and the custard and keep them warm.

5 To serve, uncover the pudding and carefully run a knife around the edge of the basin. Cover with an inverted plate and turn it out. Pour over some of the hot butterscotch sauce and serve cut into wedges with the custard and the rest of the sauce.

SERVES 10-12

1 quantity Sweet pastry
(see page 41)
6 medium eggs, beaten
3 large lemons
250 g (9 oz) caster sugar
150 ml (5 fl oz) double cream

1 Roll the pastry out thinly on a lightly floured surface and use to line a lightly greased, 25 cm (10 in), loose-bottomed flan tin, 4 cm (1½ in) deep. Prick the base here and there with a fork and chill for 20-30 minutes.

2 Preheat the oven to 200°C/400°F/Gas Mark 6. Line the pastry case with crumpled greaseproof paper, cover the base with a thin layer of baking beans and bake for 12-15 minutes, until the edges are biscuit-coloured. Carefully remove the paper and beans and return the pastry case to the oven for 3-4 minutes. Remove, brush the inside of the case with a little of the beaten egg and return to the oven once more for 2 minutes. Remove and lower the oven temperature to 120°C/250°F/Gas Mark ½.

3 For the filling, finely grate the zest from 2 of the lemons, then squeeze out enough juice from all the fruit to give you 175 ml (6 fl oz). Beat the eggs and sugar together until just mixed but not frothy. Mix in the lemon juice and cream, pour through a sieve into a jug and stir in the lemon zest.

4 Partly pull out the oven shelf, slide in the pastry case and pour in the filling. Slide the shelf back in and bake the tart for 40-45 minutes, until just set – the mixture should still be quite wobbly in the centre but it will continue to firm up after it comes out of the oven. Remove and leave to cool, but don't refrigerate it. This tart is best served on the day it is made.

SERVES 8
300 ml (10 fl oz)
full-cream milk
750 ml (1¼ pints)
double cream
6 large egg yolks
2 rounded tablespoons
cornflour
4 tablespoons caster sugar
1 x 450 g (1 lb) Madeira cake
4 tablespoons good-quality
raspberry jam
6 tablespoons Oloroso
(sweet) sherry

1 For the custard, bring the milk and 300 ml (10 fl oz) of the cream to the boil in a non-stick saucepan. Beat the egg yolks, cornflour and sugar together in a bowl, then gradually whisk in the hot milk and cream. Return the mixture to the pan and cook over a low heat, stirring constantly, for about 10 minutes, until the mixture has thickened enough to coat the back of the spoon. Take care not to let it boil or it will curdle. Transfer the custard to a bowl and leave to cool.

2 Cut the Madeira cake into slices 1 cm (½ in) thick and arrange a single layer over the base of a serving bowl, preferably glass. Spread the layer with 2 tablespoons of the raspberry jam and lay another layer of cake on top (you might not need to use all the cake). Spread the second layer with the remaining raspberry jam and sprinkle over the sherry.

3 Pour the custard over the cake, cover with cling film and chill for at least 3 hours. Whip the remaining cream into soft peaks. Uncover the trifle, spoon over the cream and return it to the fridge until you are ready to serve.

white wine syllabub

SERVES 6

**Finely grated zest and juice
of 1 large lemon
2 tablespoons brandy
50 g (2 oz) caster or
icing sugar
150 ml (5 fl oz) medium-dry
spicy white wine, such as
Gewürztraminer
300 ml (10 fl oz) double cream
Sponge fingers, to serve**

1 Mix the lemon zest and juice, brandy, sugar and white wine together in a bowl. Cover and chill for at least an hour.

2 The next day, strain the wine mixture, discarding the lemon zest. Put the cream into a bowl and begin to whisk, slowly adding the wine mixture, until the cream loosely holds its shape and leaves a ribbon on the surface when trailed from the whisk. Don't be tempted to whisk for too long or it will curdle.

3 Spoon the syllabub into tall glasses or small cups and leave somewhere cool until you are ready to serve. They can be decorated with a small twist of lemon peel, if you wish. Serve with sponge fingers.

caramelised **bread-and-butter pudding**

6-7 thin slices of white bread, crusts removed

50 g (2 oz) butter

100 g (4 oz) sultanas

250 ml (8 fl oz) double cream

250 ml (8 fl oz) full-cream milk

3 medium eggs

50 g (2 oz) caster sugar

1 vanilla pod

25 g (1 oz) icing sugar

25 g (1 oz) apricot jam, warmed and sieved

Clotted cream, to serve (optional)

1 Preheat the oven to 190°C/375°F/Gas Mark 5. Generously spread the slices of bread with the butter and then cut each slice into 4 triangles. Arrange a layer of the bread over the base of a buttered 1.5 litre (2½ pint) shallow ovenproof dish, about 6 cm (2½ in) deep. Sprinkle over the sultanas and then arrange the remaining bread triangles on top.

2 Mix the cream, milk, eggs and sugar together and pass through a sieve. Slit open the vanilla pod, scrape out the seeds and whisk them into the custard. Pour the custard over the bread and leave to soak for 5 minutes.

3 Put the dish in a roasting tin and pour enough hot water into the tin to come half way up the sides of the dish. Bake for about 30 minutes, until the top is golden and the custard has slightly set and is still quite soft in the centre. Remove the dish from the roasting tin and leave to cool for about 15 minutes. Preheat the grill to its highest setting.

4 Dust the top of the pudding heavily with icing sugar and glaze under the grill until golden. If it starts to 'soufflé' (puff up), remove from the grill and let it cool a little longer before returning to the heat. Brush the top with the sieved apricot jam and serve with some clotted cream, if you wish.

SERVES 6–8

300 g (11 oz) black rice
A small pinch of salt
750 ml (1¼ pints)
full-cream milk
1.25 litres (2¼ pints) water
2 slices of peeled fresh ginger
225 g (8 oz) light
muscovado sugar
400 ml (14 oz) can coconut
milk, chilled, to serve

FOR THE MANGO SORBET
Juice of 2 lemons
200 g (7 oz) caster sugar
75 g (3 oz) liquid glucose
3 ripe mangoes, weighing
about 450 g (1 lb) each
(or 600 ml/1 pint canned
mango pulp)

1 For the mango sorbet, make the lemon juice up to 300 ml (10 fl oz) with cold water. Put the juice, sugar and liquid glucose into a pan and bring slowly to the boil, stirring occasionally to dissolve the sugar. Remove from the heat and leave to cool.

2 Peel the mangoes and slice the flesh away from the stone. Put the flesh into a food processor and blend to a smooth purée. Stir in the lemon syrup, pass through a sieve and then churn in an ice-cream maker. Transfer to a shallow plastic container, cover and freeze until required.

3 For the black-rice pudding, put the rice into a pan with the salt, milk, water and ginger. Bring to the boil, then reduce the heat and simmer gently, stirring now and then, for 1½ hours. Add the sugar 10 minutes before the end of cooking, by which time the rice should be tender and suspended in a thick, dark purple liquid. Remove and discard the slices of ginger, transfer the rice pudding to a glass serving bowl and leave to cool.

4 Remove the mango sorbet from the freezer 10–15 minutes before you want to serve it, to allow it to soften slightly. Spoon the rice pudding into shallow serving bowls and top with a scoop of the sorbet. Pour over a little of the ice-cold coconut milk and serve straight away.

a light apple tart with quince purée

SERVES 8

900 g (2 lb) quinces (or 500 g/
1 lb 2 oz dessert apples)
100 g (4 oz) caster sugar
750 g (1½ lb) dessert apples,
such as Cox's or
Braeburns
500 g (1 lb 2 oz) fresh
puff pastry
175 g (6 oz) apricot jam
Crème fraîche, to serve

1 Peel, quarter, core and slice the quinces and put them into a pan with 75 g (3 oz) of the sugar and 3–4 tablespoons of water. Cook over a low heat for about 20 minutes, until tender, then tip into a bowl and mash to a purée with a fork. Leave to cool. (If you are making this tart with just apples, cook the 500 g (1 lb 2 oz) apples as for the quinces, but then tip them into a sieve set over a bowl to collect the excess juices. Mash the apples to a smooth purée with a fork.)

2 Roll out the pastry on a lightly floured surface and cut out a 30 cm (12 in) circle, using a plate as a template. Lift on to a lightly greased baking sheet and prick the pastry here and there with a fork, leaving a 2.5 cm (1 in) border clear around the edge. Spread the fruit purée on top, again leaving the edge clear, and chill for at least 20 minutes.

3 Preheat the oven to 200°C/400°F/Gas Mark 6. Peel and core the apples and slice them. Arrange the slices, overlapping, in circles on top of the purée and sprinkle with the remaining sugar. Bake for 30 minutes or until the pastry is crisp and the edges of the apples are lightly browned.

4 Put the apricot jam into a small pan with 1 tablespoon of water or reserved apple cooking juices, if you have them, and warm gently. Press through a sieve into a bowl and then brush over the apples. Serve the tart warm or cold, with some crème fraîche. This tart is best served on the day it is made.

panna cotta with stewed rhubarb

SERVES 6

1 vanilla pod
300 ml (10 fl oz) double cream
300 ml (10 fl oz) milk
6 tablespoons caster sugar
2 teaspoons powdered
gelatine

FOR THE STEWED RHUBARB
350 g (12 oz) young rhubarb
225 g (8 oz) granulated sugar
250 ml (8 fl oz) water

1 For the panna cotta, split open the vanilla pod and scrape out the seeds. Put both the pod and seeds into a pan with the cream, milk and sugar and simmer for 5 minutes, then remove from the heat. Meanwhile, put 2 tablespoons of cold water in a small pan and sprinkle over the gelatine. Set aside for 5 minutes, then heat gently until clear.

2 Remove the vanilla pod from the cream and stir in the dissolved gelatine. Pour into 6 dariole moulds, cover and chill for 3 hours or until set.

3 Peel the rhubarb if it is woody, though if it is very young this shouldn't be necessary. Cut it into 2.5 cm (1 in) lengths. Put the sugar and water into a pan and leave over a low heat until the sugar has completely dissolved. Bring to the boil and boil for 2 minutes, then stir in the prepared rhubarb and simmer for 1–2 minutes, until only just tender. Cover and leave to cool.

4 To serve, unmould the panna cotta on to serving plates and spoon some of the rhubarb alongside with a little of the syrup.

basic recipes

basic shortcrust pastry

MAKES ABOUT 350 G (12 OZ)
225 g (8 oz) plain flour
½ teaspoon salt
50 g (2 oz) chilled butter, cut into pieces
50 g (2 oz) chilled lard, cut into small pieces
1½–2 tablespoons cold water

rich shortcrust pastry

MAKES ABOUT 350 G (12 OZ)
225 g (8 oz) plain flour
½ teaspoon salt
65 g (2½ oz) chilled butter, cut into pieces
65 g (2½ oz) chilled lard, cut into pieces
1½–2 tablespoons cold water

1 For each type of shortcrust pastry, sift the flour and salt into a food processor or a mixing bowl. Add the pieces of chilled butter and lard and work together until the mixture looks like fine breadcrumbs.

2 Stir in the water with a round-bladed knife until the mixture comes together into a ball, turn out on to a lightly floured work surface and knead briefly until smooth. Roll out on a little more flour and use as required.

sweet pastry

MAKES ABOUT 350 G (12 OZ)
175 g (6 oz) plain flour
A small pinch of salt
50 g (2 oz) icing sugar
100 g (4 oz) chilled butter, cut into pieces
1 egg yolk
1–1½ teaspoons cold water

1 Sift the flour, salt and icing sugar into a food processor or bowl. Add the pieces of chilled butter and work together briefly, either in the food processor or with your fingertips, until the mixture looks like fine breadcrumbs.

2 Stir in the egg yolk and enough water until the mixture starts to come together into a ball (or add to the processor and process briefly), then turn out on to a lightly floured surface and knead briefly until smooth. Use as required.

custard

MAKES ABOUT 600 ML (1 PINT)
1 vanilla pod
600 ml (1 pint) full-cream milk
4 egg yolks
3 tablespoons caster sugar
4 teaspoons cornflour

1 Slit open the vanilla pod and scrape out the seeds with the tip of a sharp knife. Put the milk, vanilla pod and seeds into a non-stick pan and bring to the boil. Remove the pan from the heat and set aside for 20 minutes or so to allow the flavour of vanilla to infuse the milk.

2 Cream the egg yolks, sugar and cornflour together in a bowl until smooth. Bring the milk back to the boil, remove the vanilla pod and gradually beat the milk into the egg-yolk mixture.

3 Return to the pan and cook over a medium heat, stirring constantly, until the custard thickens, but don't let the mixture boil.

butterscotch sauce

MAKES ABOUT 450 ML (15 FL OZ)
50 g (2 oz) butter
75 g (3 oz) light muscovado sugar
25 g (1 oz) demerara sugar
150 g (5 oz) golden syrup
150 ml (5 fl oz) double cream

Put the butter, muscovado and demerara sugars and golden syrup into a pan and leave over a low heat, stirring now and then, until the sugars have dissolved. Stir in the double cream and keep warm.

chocolate sauce

MAKES ABOUT 300 ML (½ PINT)
200 ml (7 fl oz) double cream
90 g (3½ oz) good-quality plain chocolate, broken into small pieces

Put the cream and chocolate pieces into a small pan and stir over a low heat until the chocolate has melted and the sauce is silky smooth. Keep warm over a very low heat.

Liquid volume measures

1 teaspoon = 5 ml

1 tablespoon (UK/US) = 3 teaspoons = 15 ml

1 tablespoon (AUS) = 4 teaspoons = 20 ml

Note: tablespoon sizes in this book are UK/US, so Australian readers should measure 3 teaspoons where 1 tablespoon is specified in a recipe.

2 fl oz (¼ cup) = 50 ml

4 fl oz (½ cup) = 125 ml

1 cup (8 fl oz) = 250 ml

1 US pint (16 fl oz) = 450 ml

1 UK/AUS pint (20 fl oz) = 600 ml

Cup measures

Cup measurements, which are used by cooks in Australia and America, vary from ingredient to ingredient. You can use kitchen scales to measure solid/dry ingredients, or follow this handy selection of cup measurements for recipes in this book.

almonds, ground 50 g (2 oz) = ⅓ cup

butter 25 g (1 oz) = 2 tablespoons (UK/US); 50 g (2 oz) = ¼ cup; 65 g (2½ oz) = ¼ cup + 1 tablespoon; 75 g (3 oz) = ⅜ cup; 100g (4 oz) = ½ cup; 175 g (6 oz) = ¾ cup; 225 g (8 oz) = 1 cup

flour, plain 25 g (1 oz) = ¼ cup; 50g (2 oz) = ½ cup; 60 g (2¼ oz) = ½ cup + 1 tablespoon; 75 g (3 oz) = ¾ cup; 95 g (3¾ oz) = 1 cup less 1 tablespoon; 175 g (6 oz) = 1½ cups; 225 g (8 oz) = 2 cups

flour, self-raising 175 g (6 oz) = 1½ cups all-purpose flour + 2¼ teaspoons baking powder + ¾ teaspoon salt

glucose, liquid 75 g (3 oz) = ¼ cup

jam, apricot 25 g (1 oz) = 1½ tablespoons; 175 g (6 oz) = ½ cup

lard see butter

rhubarb, chopped 350 g (12 oz) = 1½ cups

rice, black 300 g (11 oz) = 1⅜ cups

sugar, caster 50 g (2 oz) = ¼ cup; 75 g (3 oz) = ⅜ cup; 100 g (4 oz) = ½ cup; 175 g (6 oz) = ¾ cup; 200 g (7 oz) = 1 cup less 2 tablespoons; 225 g (8 oz) = 1 cup; 250g (9 oz) = 1 cup + 2 tablespoons; 350 g (12 oz) = 1½ cups

sugar, demerara 25 g (1 oz) = 2 tablespoons, firmly packed

sugar, icing 25 g (1 oz) = ¼ cup; 50 g (2 oz) = ½ cup

sugar, light soft brown 50 g (2 oz) = ¼ cup, firmly packed

sugar, light muscovado 75 g (3 oz) = ⅜ cup, firmly packed; 175 g (6 oz) = ¾ cup, firmly packed; 225 g (8 oz) = 1 cup, firmly packed

sultanas 100 g (4 oz) = ⅔ cup

walnut pieces 225 g (8 oz) = 2 cups

Useful equivalents for American and Australian readers

apples, dessert such as Gala, Braeburn, Granny Smith or similar

cornflour cornstarch

cream, clotted Devonshire cream; if unavailable, substitute heavy cream

cream, double (48% butterfat) whipping or heavy cream

cream, single (min. 18% butterfat) light or table cream

crème fraîche sour cream

dariole mould baking mould shaped like a yoghurt container.

eggs, medium (UK/AUS) large (US)

flour, plain all-purpose flour

gelatine, powdered unflavoured (plain granulated) gelatin

glucose, liquid substitute equal amounts of corn syrup

golden syrup corn syrup

Madeira cake pound cake (or similar made with butter, sugar, eggs and flour)

milk, full-cream whole milk

ramekin a small individual baking dish that resembles a miniature soufflé dish

rice, black a short-grain rice, which turns a beautiful indigo when cooked; substitute risotto rice if unavailable

sherry, Oloroso a cream or sweet sherry

sponge fingers sponge cake, or ladyfingers

sugar, caster a fine-grained sugar; substitute berry sugar or granulated sugar

sugar, demerara golden brown sugar

sugar, light muscovado golden brown sugar

sugar, light soft brown golden brown sugar

sultanas golden raisins

treacle, black blackstrap molasses

vanilla pod if unavailable, substitute 1 teaspoon vanilla extract

index

The Seafood Restaurant
Riverside
Padstow
Cornwall PL28 8BY

T 01841 532 700
E for table and room bookings:
reservations@rickstein.com

St Petroc's Hotel and Bistro
4 New Street
Padstow
Cornwall PL28 8EA

contact details as for
The Seafood Restaurant

Rick Stein's Café
10 Middle Street
Padstow
Cornwall PL28 8AP

contact details as for
The Seafood Restaurant

Stein's Fish & Chips
Waterfront Business Units
South Quay
Padstow
Cornwall PL28 8BL

contact details as for
The Seafood Restaurant

Stein's Gift Shop
8 Middle Street
Padstow
Cornwall PL28 8AP

T 01841 532 221
F 01841 533 566
E reservations@rickstein.com

Mail order:
T 01841 533 250
F 01841 533 132
E mailorder@rickstein.com

Stein's Patisserie
1 Lanadwell Street
Padstow
Cornwall PL28 8AN

contact details as for
The Seafood Restaurant

Stein's Deli
Waterfront Business Units
South Quay
Padstow
Cornwall PL28 8BL

contact details as for
The Seafood Restaurant

Padstow Seafood School
Waterfront Business Units
South Quay
Padstow
Cornwall PL28 8BL

T 01841 533 466
F 01841 533 344
E seafoodschool@rickstein.com

Website for all information:
www.rickstein.com